QuoteOctopus.com

The best quotes

Publisher Contact

257 Swanston Street, Melbourne, VIC, AUSTRALIA

Email: hello@quoteoctopus.com

Social media: facebook.com/quoteoctopus

Acknowledgements

The team at Quote Octopus would like to thank our friends, family, suppliers and customers for making our vision of creating the highest-quality books a reality. Thanks for purchasing and enjoy the quotes!

This page is intentionally left blank

This page is intentionally left blank

A vote of confidence from Cisco Systems can be very important to fledging technology companies, especially if they have initial public offerings on the horizon.

Alex Berenson

Accounting rules give financial institutions flexibility about when they choose to recognize venture capital profits.

Alex Berenson

African runners regularly work out in the United States and Europe, and the International Olympic Committee sends some of the cash from the Games to Olympic committees in poor nations, which use the money to finance their own programs.

Alex Berenson

After a generation of misrule under Mr. Hussein, who built a huge military infrastructure while neglecting civilian investment, and a dozen years of United Nations sanctions, Iraq's unemployment rate tops 50 percent.

Alex Berenson

Also, most people read fiction as an escape - and I wonder whether my books aren't a bit too grounded in reality to reach the widest possible audience.

Alex Berenson

Although not well known outside Wall Street, Freddie Mac and its corporate cousin, Fannie Mae, are two of the world's largest financial institutions and play a crucial role in the housing market.

Alex Berenson

America Online, of course, is a master of the hard sell, from stuffing mailboxes with free trial offers to forcing subscribers to click through ads before they can get their e-mail.

Alex Berenson

An attack on the scale of Sept. 11 would rock the markets and the economy.

Alex Berenson

As a public servant, William H. Webster has an impeccable resume.

Alex Berenson

As a reporter, I embedded for modest stints with American soldiers in Afghanistan and Iraq. When I'm asked about those experiences, I always say - and mean - that we civilians don't deserve the soldiers we have.

Alex Berenson

As the Nasdaq soared in 1999 and early 2000, demand for many offerings far exceeded the supply of shares available at the initial offering price.

Alex Berenson

As they grow, companies saturate their markets, become more complex and difficult to manage, and face larger and more entrenched competitors.

Alex Berenson

At any moment, one company stands in the spotlight of the middle ring in the stock market's never-ending circus. It may not be the biggest corporation in the world, or the most profitable, but somehow it both mirrors and leads the market's broader action.

Alex Berenson

At first glance, Martha Stewart, queen of artfully distressed home furnishings, might not seem to have much in common with Michael R. Milken, one-time king of junk bonds.

Alex Berenson

At the end of 2000, most investors were optimistic that a return to quick gains could not be far off.

Alex Berenson

Automated call centers are only the most obvious way speech recognition will be used. The software is now becoming sophisticated enough to identify speakers through 'voiceprints,' akin to fingerprints, eventually reducing the need for personal identification numbers.

Alex Berenson

Because Genentech is a leading developer of cancer therapies, some doctors also fear that the company's pricing plans for Avastin - around $8,800 a month - may encourage other companies to charge more for their own oncology drugs.

Alex Berenson

Before Jason Bourne, before Jack Ryan, there was Bond, James Bond, the original two-dimensional, world-saving secret agent.

Alex Berenson

Benefits are rarely made public in filings with the Securities and Exchange Commission, where companies must report the pay and options that their five highest-paid executives receive.

Alex Berenson

Big banks have long had private equity divisions that put up capital for deals too complex or risky for individual shareholders to finance.

Alex Berenson

Big companies often use their leverage to take stakes in would-be suppliers, especially in the technology business.

Alex Berenson

Big companies, which spend tens of billions of dollars annually on 'call centers' to take orders and provide customer support, increasingly rely on speech recognition not just to handle requests for information but to process customer orders.

Alex Berenson

Big fund companies have many ways to increase the returns of young funds that they want to promote. And at least one of those games involves popular offerings.

Alex Berenson

Big swings in the wholesale price of electricity are not unusual in the summer, when high demand taxes generators' ability to supply power.

Alex Berenson

Bigger spreads mean bigger gaps between what buyers pay and sellers receive. For example, a spread of 10 cents a share means that the buyer pays $100 more for 1,000 shares than the seller receives.

Alex Berenson

Business cycles lengthened greatly during the 20th century, as central banks learned to manage national economies by raising and lowering interest rates.

Alex Berenson

Climate change might be disastrous, but does that mean we want carbon taxes that raise the price of a gallon of heating oil to $10? And how exactly will those taxes affect economic growth?

Alex Berenson

Companies buy customers when they cannot win new business on their own. They merge when their executives do not have a better idea of what to do.

Alex Berenson

Corporate executives often buy or sell shares in their companies, and stocks rarely rise or fall significantly when those transactions are reported.

Alex Berenson

Determining how many asbestos suits have been filed or how much companies have spent to resolve them is difficult. Cases are filed in state and federal courts, and many companies do not disclose their spending on settlements.

Alex Berenson

Did anyone in the White House or the N.S.A or the C.I.A. consider flying to Hong Kong and treating Mr. Snowden like a human being, offering him a chance to testify before Congress and a fair trial?

Alex Berenson

Don't expect Barton Biggs to be offering his market insights on 'Bloomberg News' anytime soon. His plumber, maybe.

Alex Berenson

Downhill track sports like luge are technology battles, as exciting as a NASCAR qualifying day.

Alex Berenson

Economics pretends to be a science. Its practitioners fill blackboards with equations and clog computers with data. But it is really a faith, or more accurately a set of overlapping and squabbling faiths, each with its own doctrines.

Alex Berenson

Electronic communications networks match trades between investors directly, without using a market maker or specialist as an intermediary.

Alex Berenson

Enron Field in Houston, the Trans World Dome in St. Louis and PSINet Stadium in Baltimore are just three of the modern-day coliseums named for companies that have found new homes in bankruptcy court.

Alex Berenson

Enron had already collapsed and filed for bankruptcy protection by the beginning of 2002. But despite complaints from short sellers that corporations had used accounting gimmickry to inflate their profits, many investors thought the crisis at Enron was an isolated case.

Alex Berenson

Equity is the cushion that protects financial institutions from unexpected changes in the value of their assets. The greater the leverage, the smaller the losses required to wipe out a company's equity, leaving it without enough money to repay the people who hold its debt.

Alex Berenson

Even a war zone looks peaceful in most places, most of the time.

Alex Berenson

Even so, sometimes I wish I did have a little bit more flair in my language.

Alex Berenson

Even technology companies get good news sometimes.

Alex Berenson

Every public company depends to some extent on the trust of its investors.

Alex Berenson

Evidence of defendants' lavish lifestyles is often used to provide a motive for fraud. Jurors sometimes wonder why an executive making tens of millions of dollars would cheat to make even more. Evidence of habitual gluttony helps provide the answer.

Alex Berenson

Fannie Mae has never publicly disclosed how much money it could lose if interest rates rose 1.5 percentage points in a very short period of time.

Alex Berenson

Fannie Mae is owned by shareholders but operates under a federal charter that exempts it from paying state or local taxes. As a result, many professional investors think the government would repay the debt that Fannie Mae had issued if the company could not, although Fannie Mae explicitly says that its bonds do not carry a federal guarantee.

Alex Berenson

Federal laws against kickbacks bar pharmaceutical companies from directly giving money to patients for co-payments on the drugs they make.

Alex Berenson

Financial news services and other media organizations get press releases 15 minutes before they are distributed to the general public, fueling a furious competition among the news services to rewrite them for their subscribers during their window of exclusivity.

Alex Berenson

For a developing country, average long-run growth of 5 percent a year per capita is excellent, and 7 percent is stellar.

Alex Berenson

For a spy novelist like me, the Edward J. Snowden story has everything. A man driven by ego and idealism - can anyone ever distinguish the two? - leaves his job and his beautiful girlfriend behind. He must tell the world the Panopticon has arrived. His masters vow to punish him, and he heads for Moscow in a desperate search for refuge.

Alex Berenson

For as long as anyone can remember, reliable, cheap electricity has been taken for granted in the United States.

Alex Berenson

For chat-room tyros who expect to make their first million day-trading by age 27, paging through the Sunday newspaper with a pair of scissors just to save a couple of cents on Cheetos seems so, well, old economy.

Alex Berenson

For decades, Wall Street has charged companies a standard fee of 7 percent to sell their shares to the public.

Alex Berenson

For investors who do want to speculate in high-yield bonds, one alternative may be a junk bond mutual fund, which can offer investors the relative safety of diversification.

Alex Berenson

For more than two decades, Barry Diller has been among the most respected - and feared - figures in the entertainment industry.

Alex Berenson

For value investors, General Motors is a tempting target. The company's share of the North American auto market has steadily declined for two decades, and analysts say the company suffers from weak management and unexciting cars.

Alex Berenson

For years, critics of Fannie Mae have warned that it does not give them enough information to judge its risks.

Alex Berenson

From 1983 to 2000, William Goren stole more than $30 million from investors on Long Island and in Queens. His favorite targets were widows and retired couples, like Helga and Simon Novack, Holocaust survivors who gave Mr. Goren their life savings.

Alex Berenson

Generally, a rally will have staying power, technicians say, if, in addition to price movements, it has heavy trading volume and breadth, meaning that several stocks rise for each stock that falls.

Alex Berenson

Good spectator sports share certain fundamentals. Their competitors battle head-to-head. Their winners are determined objectively: fastest runner, most points. They are refereed, not judged.

Alex Berenson

HealthWell is just one of several foundations that assist patients in making their insurance co-payments for expensive drugs.

Alex Berenson

Hedge funds try to produce above-average investment returns using tactics ranging from traditional stock-picking to complex derivative and arbitrage plays. High minimum investments, redemption restrictions and aggressive strategies make them suitable mainly for more sophisticated and well-heeled investors.

Alex Berenson

Higher productivity enables companies to increase sales without adding workers. Even if job markets tighten and wages rise, corporate profits can continue to climb as long as worker productivity is growing faster than overall wages.

Alex Berenson

I know it's a cliche, but trust me on this. I once dated a Canadian. Canada = boring.

Alex Berenson

I think in some ways what Snowden is, is he's a mix of a cold war spy novel and post-9/11 spy novel.

Alex Berenson

I think when you have lawyers arguing over whether you can keep a detainee at 46 degrees... for two hours, that's not torture. It may be unpleasant, it may be coercive... but let's say what torture actually is, and that's not it.

Alex Berenson

If only the human body could handle trauma as well as biotechnology stocks do.

Alex Berenson

In Ghazalia, Mr. Hussein showed his contempt for the majority Shiites in ways large and small. He refused to allow them even one mosque, while the Sunnis had nearly a dozen. To worship, the Shiites had to cross an inconveniently located bridge over the sewage canal to Shula.

Alex Berenson

In a Ponzi scheme, a promoter pays back his initial investors with money he has raised from new investors. Eventually, the promoter can no longer find enough new investors to pay off the people who have already put up money, and the scheme collapses.

Alex Berenson

In general, great companies prefer to grow 'organically,' as Wall Street likes to say. That is, from the inside out, by finding new markets or by taking market share from their competitors.

Alex Berenson

In general, investors prefer companies to reward executives for producing recurring income, not one-time gains.

Alex Berenson

In market valuation, Yahoo is worth about as much Walt Disney and the News Corporation combined.

Alex Berenson

In the short run, using militias might be the quickest and easiest way to improve order on Iraq's streets and uproot the terrorists and guerrillas who routinely attack American troops and civilian targets.

Alex Berenson

Individual income can grow only as fast as productivity rises.

Alex Berenson

Information technology departments must spend enormous amounts of time and money worrying about integrating big computer systems with billions of pieces of customer data.

Alex Berenson

Insider trading is hard to prove. To be convicted, a person must have bought or sold a stock based on material information that is both unknown to the general public and likely to have had an important effect on a company's stock price.

Alex Berenson

Institutions like mutual funds often worry that if they disclose their plans to buy a stock, copycats will move quickly and drive up the stock before the purchase is completed.

Alex Berenson

Investors have been too willing to buy stocks with strong reported earnings, even if they do not understand how the earnings are produced.

Alex Berenson

Iraq is short on capital, short on electricity, and short on management expertise, but it does not lack economic enthusiasm.

Alex Berenson

It has been said that the Fed's job is to take the punch bowl away just as the party gets going, raising interest rates when the economy is growing too fast and inflation threatens.

Alex Berenson

It is a truth universally acknowledged on Wall Street that original research is on life support. Serious research can be bad for business, as well as expensive.

Alex Berenson

It's no secret that big institutional investors have a lot of advantages on Wall Street. They get the first chance to buy hot initial public offerings. They get to meet in person with companies' managements.

Alex Berenson

It's one of the fundamental principles of the stock market: When interest rates go up, stocks go down. And along with financial companies and cyclicals, technology companies - with their sky-high price-to-earnings multiples - should be among the biggest losers in an environment of rising rates.

Alex Berenson

John W. Snow was paid more than $50 million in salary, bonus and stock in his nearly 12 years as chairman of the CSX Corporation, the railroad company. During that period, the company's profits fell, and its stock rose a bit more than half as much as that of the average big company.

Alex Berenson

Like many other banks and finance companies, Green Tree used a process called securitization to resell its home loans to outside investors. Green Tree grouped thousands of these small loans into a pool worth hundreds of millions of dollars.

Alex Berenson

Lower interest rates are usually considered good for stocks because they lower the cost of borrowing and make bonds a less attractive alternative investment.

Alex Berenson

Macroeconomics is the analysis of the economy as a whole, an examination of overall supply and demand. At the broadest level, macroeconomists want to understand why some countries grow faster than others and which government policies can help growth.

Alex Berenson

Many legal experts note that prosecutors regularly seek indictments of people or companies for destroying evidence or impeding investigations, even if they cannot prove other charges.

Alex Berenson

Many newly public companies are able to post a year or two of strong sales growth off a small base, but their growth almost always slows over time, thanks to what investment professionals call 'the law of large numbers.'

Alex Berenson

Microeconomics is the study of how specific choices made by businesses, consumers and governments affect the markets for different goods and services. For example, a microeconomist might examine how price changes affect sales of apples relative to oranges.

Alex Berenson

Most companies can survive even if their debt ratings are lowered below investment grade, although they will have higher borrowing costs.

Alex Berenson

Most of America never noticed, but the 1990s were good times for trailer homes, a.k.a. manufactured housing. From 1991 to

1998, annual sales of manufactured homes more than doubled, to 374,000 from 174,000.

Alex Berenson

Most unfortunately, Enron's plunge into bankruptcy court also cost many of its rank-and-file employees their savings.

Alex Berenson

Mr. Hussein began building Ghazalia in the early 1980s as a home for army officers and other members of his Baath Party. Concrete mansions with pillars and domes are common in the southern half of the district.

Alex Berenson

Mr. Snowden did not start out as a spy, and calling him one bends the term past recognition. Spies don't give their secrets to journalists for free.

Alex Berenson

Never underestimate the power of Abby Joseph Cohen.

Alex Berenson

Normally, banks record profits on loans only as they are repaid, whether they securitize the loans or hold them on their books.

Alex Berenson

Of all the big Internet companies, Yahoo is the most highly valued on a price-earnings and price-sales basis.

Alex Berenson

Of course, the discounting of future earnings should hurt all stocks. But it should hurt technology stocks more than others, because so many of them are valued at extremely high levels relative to their current earnings.

Alex Berenson

On the New York Stock Exchange, all buy and sell orders are routed through a single 'specialist,' guaranteeing that most small trades can be matched directly. But most larger trades are delivered to the specialist on the floor of the exchange by human brokers, a system that big investors view as increasingly inefficient.

Alex Berenson

One of the Internet's highest-profile companies, Priceline once dreamed of transforming the way consumer goods are bought and sold by offering customers the chance to 'name your own price' for a variety of products, including airline tickets.

Alex Berenson

Over the years, I've spent time in Saudi Arabia, the Bekaa Valley, Afghanistan, Jordan, and Kenya, among other vacation hotspots.

Alex Berenson

Plumbing is usually boring.

Alex Berenson

Predicting the market is always tough.

Alex Berenson

Publicly traded United States companies report sales and profits to investors every quarter.

Alex Berenson

Rising interest rates are considered bad for stocks because they raise the cost of doing business and depress corporate earnings and because higher yields make bonds relatively more attractive than stocks to investors.

Alex Berenson

Robert M. Morgenthau, the Manhattan district attorney, has seen a few financial schemes in his time. As the lead local prosecutor in the world's financial capital, he has battled frauds like the Bank of Credit and Commerce International, which stole billions of dollars from investors worldwide.

Alex Berenson

Sergeant Bergdahl may have broken any number of military laws.

Alex Berenson

Shareholder meetings are not usually the occasion for utter candor - or for that matter, arch sarcasm - by chief executives.

Alex Berenson

Short sellers sell stock they have borrowed, hoping to buy it back later when its price has fallen.

Alex Berenson

Sochi started with the same problem as every Winter Olympics. Forget the crass commercialism, the fake amateurism, NBC's refusal to televise important events live to all its viewers. As an event, the Winter Games fail on the most basic level. They're lousy to watch.

Alex Berenson

Soldiers willingly, sometimes foolishly, risk their own lives to keep their comrades out of enemy hands.

Alex Berenson

Some big banks remain wary of venture capital.

Alex Berenson

Some companies use off-balance-sheet partnerships to raise money or to buy assets without ever telling their shareholders in their financial statements.

Alex Berenson

Stocks in the United States plunged in 2002 amid fears of war and terrorism, a weak economy, rising oil prices and dozens of corporate scandals. It was the third consecutive annual decline, the first time that has happened in 60 years.

Alex Berenson

Studies show that Avastin can prolong the lives of patients with late-stage breast and lung cancer by several months when the drug is combined with existing therapies.

Alex Berenson

Technology investment drove growth in the 1990s, both directly and by fueling a rising stock market that led to increased consumer spending.

Alex Berenson

The American pledge not to negotiate with terrorists has been honored more in the breach than the observance from the moment President Ronald Reagan made it.

Alex Berenson

The Fed's ability to raise and lower short-term interest rates is its primary control over the economy.

Alex Berenson

The Wahhabists are the boogeymen, the guys who will chop the head off any American they catch. And they will destroy Iraq without a second thought if they believe that the instability will benefit them.

Alex Berenson

The biggest profit center for investment banks is the hefty fees they charge for underwriting stock offerings and giving financial advice, and analysts put those profits at risk if they publish negative conclusions about the companies that pay the fees.

Alex Berenson

The credit quality of junk bonds varies widely.

Alex Berenson

The details of the personal expenses that executives put on the company tab often are not known because loopholes in federal disclosure rules let publicly traded companies generally avoid disclosing the perks they give executives along with pay and stock options.

Alex Berenson

The difference between microeconomics and macroeconomics is a bit like the difference between biology and medicine. Knowing that certain genes increase the risk of cancer is relatively easy. Figuring out exactly which people will get sick, or how to cure them, is a lot more complicated.

Alex Berenson

The fact that we haven't faced another major terrorist attack on American soil since Sept. 11 is a very significant achievement, and one that's easy to forget - it's the dog that doesn't bark.

Alex Berenson

The lower spreads mean lower costs for investors, because Nasdaq investors generally do not trade directly with one another. Instead, they usually buy and sell from market-makers, brokerage firms that flip shares between buyers and sellers and keep the spread for themselves.

Alex Berenson

The market always, in theory at least, looks ahead. And it's always trying to take in every bit of information that it can as quickly as it can. You don't really care so much if the company made a dollar last year; you want to know what it's going to make this year.

Alex Berenson

The most distinguishing element of my novels is that I try as hard as I can - within the context of a popular commercial thriller - to make them feel authentic. Drawing on real locations and real events is part of that authenticity.

Alex Berenson

The notion that employees and companies have a social contract with each other that goes beyond a paycheck has largely vanished in United States business.

Alex Berenson

The stock prices of networking equipment companies like Cisco Systems and Nortel Networks sometimes seem as if they are priced for perpetual success.

Alex Berenson

The thing to do with mutual funds is to buy a couple of decent ones, set up an investment plan and then never, ever think about them again, except maybe once a quarter or so when you take a peek at your statements to make sure that you have not accidentally been buying the Fidelity Peace-in-the-Middle-East fund.

Alex Berenson

The world is filled with great sporting events.

Alex Berenson

To economists, prices serve as crucial signals to producers and consumers. In a regulated market, the state sets prices high enough for private companies to cover their costs and earn a guaranteed profit for their investors. But in a deregulated market, prices should vary with demand and supply.

Alex Berenson

To finance deficits, the government must sell bonds to investors, competing for capital that could otherwise be used to invest in stocks or corporate bonds. Government borrowings raise long-term interest rates, stifling economic growth.

Alex Berenson

Traditionally, companies have made major announcements before or after the close of trading so that all interested investors and analysts are apprised of the news before trading resumes in their stocks.

Alex Berenson

Trailer home borrowers, mostly near the bottom of the economic ladder, often default on their loans.

Alex Berenson

Trust the Canadians to produce a game about mutual funds that is actually more boring than the real thing.

Alex Berenson

Trust-me companies are companies whose financial results gallop ahead of their businesses, companies with seemingly perfect control over their quarterly sales and profits. Companies whose financial statements are loaded with footnotes: companies that short-sellers often attack but rarely dent.

Alex Berenson

Volatility may be rising simply because investors must digest more information every day.

Alex Berenson

Wal-Mart does not do big mergers, though it will buy much smaller competitors in so-called 'tuck-in acquisitions.'

Alex Berenson

What Mr. Snowden at first seemed to want - and rightly - was to force our electronic spies to answer, in plain English, 'Are you saving e-mails, Skype and other Internet communications? What about phone calls? For how long? Who can get access to this data, and is a warrant required in each case? How are calls between Americans treated?' Et cetera.

Alex Berenson

Whatever the potential pitfalls, banks are increasingly enthusiastic about venture capital, particularly in new companies with strong prospects in fields like health care and technology.

Alex Berenson

When all the plants in a region are running at full steam, there is simply no way to get more power.

Alex Berenson

While Wall Street firms typically underwrite offerings in teams, the lead underwriter, or manager, of the offering has primary responsibility for selling the offering and reaps much of the fees and profit.

Alex Berenson

With 950 reporters and 79 bureaus, Bloomberg competes to break news with Dow Jones, Reuters and Bridge News along with newspaper Web sites, dozens of smaller Internet sites, and even gossipy chat rooms.

Alex Berenson

Would-be drug companies must either produce medicines that stand up to federal scrutiny, demonstrate that their data has value to other companies, or go out of business.

Alex Berenson

This page is intentionally left blank

This page is intentionally left blank

This page is intentionally left blank

This page is intentionally left blank

This page is intentionally left blank

www.ingramcontent.com/pod-product-compliance
Lightning Source LLC
Chambersburg PA
CBHW072020290526
45787CB00013B/1442